MÁIRE NÍ CHATHASAIGH

THE IRISH HARPER
VOLUME · TWO

OLD BRIDGE MUSIC

The Irish Harper: Volume Two
Máire Ní Chathasaigh

ISBN 1 873077 01 7

Published in 2001 by
Old Bridge Music
PO Box 7
Ilkley
West Yorkshire
LS29 9RY
England

www.oldbridgemusic.com

© Máire Ní Chathasaigh 2001

The photograph of Máire Ní Chathasaigh was taken by Chris Newman
The portrait of Turlough O'Carolan is taken from *The Annals of the Irish Harpers* by Charlotte Milligan Fox (London, 1911)

Do'm athair aerach álainn, Seán Ó Cathasaigh, a d'éag imbliana

All Rights Reserved

No part of this publication may be reproduced, transmitted or stored in any form or by any means, electronic or mechanical, including photocopy, recording or any other information storage or retrieval system, without prior permission in writing from the publisher.

CONTENTS

An Introduction to Turlough O'Carolan	4
Bibliography & Further Recordings	4
Notes on Performance	5
The Music	
1. Carolan's Draught	6
2. John O'Connor	8
3. Colonel John Irwin (Planxty Irwin)	10
4. Hewlett	12
5. Blind Mary (Máire Dhall)	13
6. Lord Inchiquin	14
7. Morgan Magan	15
8. Sheebeg & Sheemore (Sí Bheag's Sí Mhór)	16
9. The Princess Royal	18
10. John Drury	20
11. Fanny Power	21
12. Carolan's Concerto	22
13. Maurice O'Connor	24
14. Constantine Maguire	25
15. Mr. O'Connor	26
16. Robert Jordan	30
17. Bridget Cruise	32
18. Frank Palmer	33
19. Grace Nugent	34
20. George Brabazon	36
21. Kean O'Hara	37
22. Madam Judge	38
23. Eleanor Plunkett	40
24. Baptist Johnston	41
Notes on the Music	
Nos. 1 – 8	9
Nos. 9 – 15	29
Nos. 16 – 24	42
Information about the associated recording *The Carolan Albums*	43
Also by Máire Ní Chathasaigh	43 – 44

Turlough O'Carolan / Toirbhealbhach Ó Cearbhalláin
Harper & Composer (1670 -1738)

Turlough O'Carolan was the most celebrated Irish harper and composer of his day, and, by the early eighteenth century, was one of the most famous men in Ireland. Edward Bunting, to whose heroic labours as a collector we owe the survival of much of Carolan's music, tells us that *"he never excelled as a performer"*, but he had the rare gift of producing melodies both popular and lasting. He was of upright character, witty and sociable, and universally popular. Over two hundred of the tunes that he composed for his friends and patrons have survived. His arrival at the house of a patron was an occasion for rejoicing, Carolan being as much sought after for his company as for his music. He composed celebratory pieces for his patrons' weddings, and composed elegies when they died. The harpers of the period insisted on a status of social equality with their patrons, and Carolan was no exception. He was on friendly terms with Jonathan Swift and many other notables of the Ireland of his time. The diarist Charles O'Conor of Belanagare (who was of very ancient princely lineage, being directly descended from the last High King of Ireland Turlough Mór O'Conor d. 1198, and whose family, together with the McDermotts of Alderford, were Carolan's principal patrons) tells us that *"he was above playing for hire"*. James Hardiman says *"he always expected, and invariably received, that attention to which...he was so eminently entitled. At the houses where he visited, he was welcomed more as a friend than as an itinerant minstrel. His visits were regarded as favours conferred, and his departure never failed to occasion regret."* Indeed, his patrons were terrified of offending him, and spared no expense in making him welcome - a welcome which was as warm in the houses of the new English settlers as it was in those of the old Gaelic aristocracy. In the former case this is particularly astonishing considering that Carolan's heyday coincided with the most repressive period of the Penal Laws and that he continued openly to adhere to the Catholic religion. Nor did Carolan make any distinction between his patrons: that is, between the dispossessed Gaels and the newcomers who had profited by the dispossessions and acquired their estates as a result of the Cromwellian confiscations. (Many of Carolan's patrons suffered very badly, as had been intended, from the provisions of the penal code in relation to inheritance and possession of property.)

Carolan was born in Nobber, Co. Meath. When he was about fourteen years old, his family moved to Co. Roscommon, where the McDermott Roes of Alderford House, Ballyfarnon, employed his father John. Mrs McDermott Roe took an interest in him and bore the cost of his education. He contracted smallpox when he was eighteen and became totally blind as a result. Mrs McDermott Roe thereupon sent him to study for three years with a harper - also named McDermott Roe - who lived nearby. She then equipped him with a horse, a guide and enough money to give him a good start, and at the age of twenty-one he embarked upon his career as a harper. Upon his marriage to Mary Maguire, a gentlewoman from Co. Fermanagh, he settled near Mohill, Co. Leitrim; they had seven children. Carolan was very fond of his wife, and composed an affecting elegy for her when she died in 1733. He himself died in his old home at Alderford five years later, on the 25th of March 1738, and is buried in the McDermott Roe family vault in Kilronan Churchyard.

Pieces 1 - 24 in this book correspond to tracks 1 - 24 of a CD **The Carolan Albums** (Old Bridge Music, 1994; OBMCD06).

Bibliography

Carolan: The Life, Times & Music of an Irish Harper by Donal O'Sullivan, published in two volumes by Routledge & Kegan Paul, London 1958; reprinted in one volume with a new Appendix containing additional material by Ossian Publications, Cork 2001.
The Ancient Music of Ireland by Edward Bunting (originally published in three volumes 1796, 1809 & 1840; re-issued by Mercier Press 1969)
The Irish Harp by Joan Rimmer (Mercier Press, 1969)
The Harp of Ireland by Gráinne Yeats, published by the Belfast Harpers' Bicentenary Ltd., 1992.
Irish Life in the Seventeenth Century by Edward McLysaght, 1939

Further Recordings

I've recorded six other Carolan pieces on various albums over the years. *Planxty Sudley, Madam Maxwell, Charles O'Conor* and *Carolan's Farewell to Music* appear on my solo album **The New Strung Harp** (Temple Records, 1985). (*Carolan's Farewell to Music* also appears on the compilation album **Bringing it All Back Home** (Hummingbird Records). *Lady Dillon* appears on my 1988 album with Chris Newman, **The Living Wood** (Old Bridge Music OBMCD07) and *Lady Gethin* appears on my 1991 album with Chris Newman, **Out of Court** (Old Bridge Music OBMCD03). Transcriptions of these have not been included in the current book as it was thought preferable that its contents should correspond exactly to those of **The Carolan Albums**.

NOTES ON PERFORMANCE

Only Carolan's melodies survive; we have little idea what sort of accompaniments he may have used. The harp arrangements in this book and on the associated recording are therefore based on an analysis of stylistic evidence within the tunes concerned. Carolan's music was quite different to that of the Irish harpers that came before. It's said that he was fond of the music of Corelli and Geminiani and many of his compositions are in a quasi-Baroque style. Others, such as *Blind Mary* and *Bridget Cruise*, are more in the style of a traditional Irish song, and others still are in the style of a traditional Irish jig. They have all been arranged accordingly. (Though it's true that Carolan was influenced by the baroque style, we have no way of knowing if he "hibernicised" it - he probably did - or whether the ornaments he used were those generally employed by European musicians of that period. Thus the styles of arrangement in this book swing from baroque to Irish to hibernicised baroque and back again.)

Since these nuances of style cannot be precisely indicated by conventional music notation, careful listening to the associated recording is strongly recommended. The suggested tempi are approximate only.

Words of Carolan's authorship survive to many of his compositions. Edward Bunting was told by one of the old harpers that *"Carolan always made the tune first and the poetry last"* and this is patently true. Many of Carolan's tunes have a range that is greater than that of the human voice and so he cannot have sung the words in the conventional sense. He may perhaps have chanted them in the manner of the *reacaire*, or professional court reciter, of previous centuries. Some of the tunes on this recording are described as "Planxties": the term "Planxty" appears to have originated with Carolan, who may have coined it himself to denote a festive harp-tune.

SYMBOLS USED IN HARP NOTATION

⌊⌋ or ⌈⌉ = place all fingers within the bracket on the strings before playing

, = lift the fingers from the strings

⌒ = cross the thumb over while keeping the previous finger on its own string, or pass the indicated finger underneath the thumb while keeping the thumb on its own string

⋰⋱ = slide the thumb directly across on to the neighbouring string, then play that string with the thumb also; or slide the fourth finger upwards on to the neighbouring string, then play that string with the fourth finger also

⊖ = open hand damping

↓ = play the arpeggio downwards. This was one of the most characteristic techniques of the old Irish harpers.

L.V. = laissez vibrer (allow the strings to vibrate)

COPYRIGHT DETAILS

The copyright in all of the arrangements in this book remains with the author. The arrangements are registered with the Mechanical Copyright Protection Society, Elgar House, 41 Streatham High Road, LONDON, SW16 1ER and with the Performing Rights Society, 29-33 Berners Street, LONDON, W1P 4AA.

If you'd like to perform these pieces publicly for profit, or to record any of them, you need to apply in the first instance to Old Bridge Music for permission. Additionally, in the case of commercial recordings, your record company needs to apply to the MCPS or one of its overseas affiliates (for example, the Harry Fox Agency in the USA) for a License to Manufacture. In the case of radio or TV performance, please ensure that the correct copyright details are given to the producer. Please note that the copyright is held in the name of Máire Ní Chathasaigh, not Old Bridge Music.

CAROLAN'S DRAUGHT

Turlough O'Carolan (1670 - 1738)
Trad. arr. © 1985 Máire Ní Chathasaigh

© 1985 Máire Ní Chathasaigh

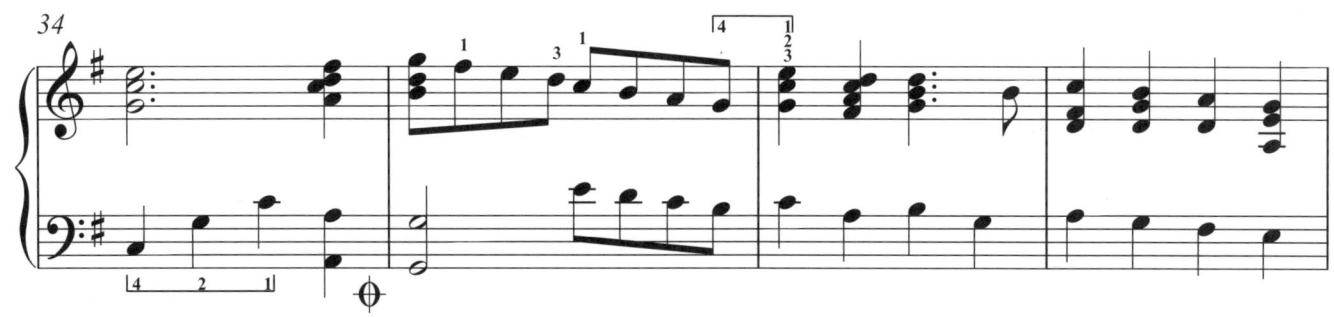
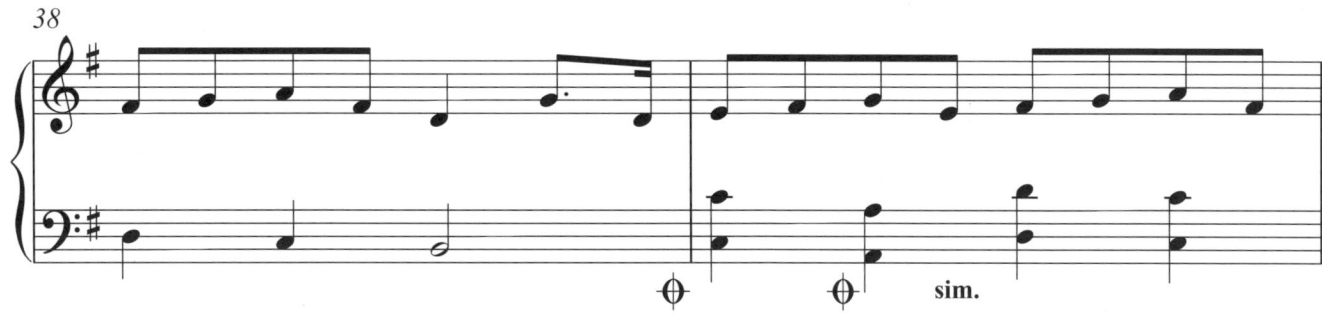

© 1985 Máire Ní Chathasaigh

D.C.

JOHN O'CONNOR

Turlough O'Carolan (1670 - 1738)
Trad. arr. © 1991 Máire Ní Chathasaigh

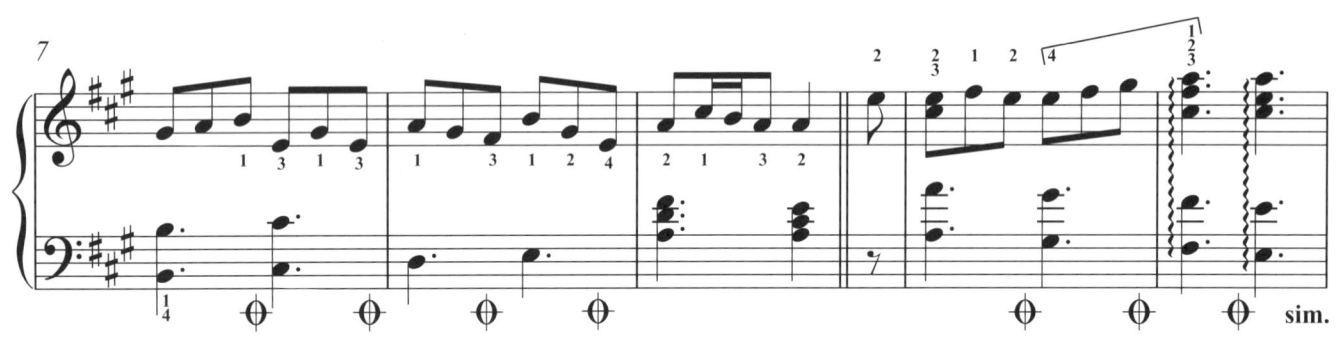
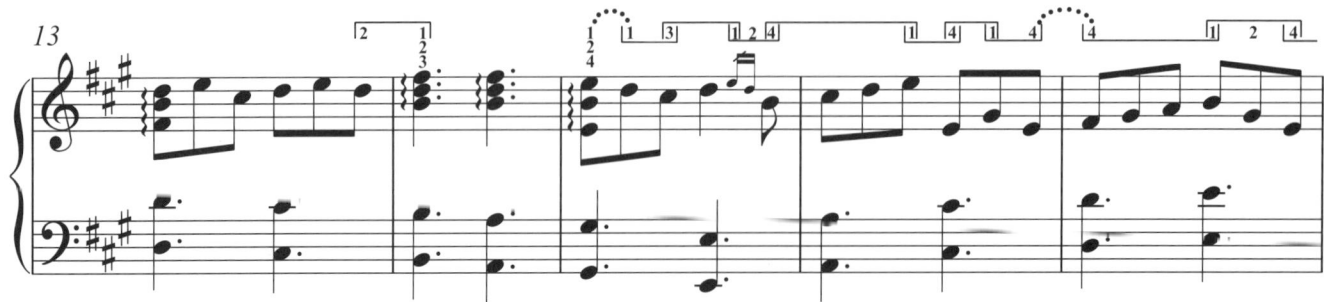

© 1991 Máire Ní Chathasaigh

1. **Carolan's Draught** (pp.6 - 7)
George Petrie tells us that he obtained this version of the tune from an old MS. music-book sent to him by a Father Walsh, Parish Priest of Sneem, Co. Kerry.

2. **John O'Connor**, or **Planxty Connor** (p.8)
Edward Bunting noted the air from the Co. Derry harper Denis Hempson. John O'Connor Faly was the head of the house of Offaly, whose principal stronghold until 1556 was Daingean Uí Fáilghe (the Fortress of Offaly) until Offaly was broken up and made shire ground as the King's County and Daingean was renamed Philipstown, both the new names being in honour of Queen Mary's husband, King Philip of Spain. John was a Counsellor-at-Law and represented Philipstown in King James's Parliament of 1689; when war broke out, he held the rank of Colonel in the King's army and was killed at the Battle of Aughrim in 1691. His son Maurice, the head of the family in Carolan's day, succeeded him. (See notes to **Maurice O'Connor**).

     William Shield, Master of the King's Music, 1817, and composer to Covent Garden Theatre, often incorporated (as was then customary in England) items by other composers in his operas and other stage pieces. He "often collaborated with John O'Keeffe, an Irishman...Their most successful opera was *The Poor Soldier* (1782), for which Shield arranged a number of Irish tunes O'Keeffe had sung to him. [This Carolan composition was one of them.] As a result Irish songs became a commonplace in English operas for the rest of the century..." - *The New Grove Dictionary of Music and Musicians*, 1980. (See also **The Princess Royal**.)

     Arthur O'Neill tells us in his Memoirs that when he was 15 years old and at the beginning of his career as a harper, he was present at High Mass in the Chapel of Navan, Co. Meath, on Christmas Day, 1752, when the harper Thady Elliott, who usually accompanied the service on his harp there, for a bet struck up **Planxty Connor** at the Elevation, the most solemn part of the Mass. This exploit created a sensation, poor Thady was dismissed and the post offered then and there to O'Neill himself, who declined it on the grounds that Thady had always been kind to him.

     The rhythm should be that of a traditional Irish jig from the oral tradition. For this and all other jig-like tunes in this book, I would strongly recommend listening to the associated recording on *The Carolan Albums*.

3. **Colonel John Irwin**, or **Planxty Irwin** (pp.10 - 11)
Obtained by Bunting from Charles Byrne, the Co. Leitrim harper. Composed for Colonel John Irwin (1680 - 1752) of Tanrego House, Ballysodare Bay, Co. Sligo, High Sheriff of Sligo in 1731. He is described in the first verse of the poem as "An t-Óigfhear Gaodhalach Gállta" ("the young Anglo-Irishman") and in the second as having acquitted himself with distinction in Flanders ("D'fhéach sé a chúrsa i bhFlanders"). We can therefore assume that the song was composed soon after the Peace of Utrecht in 1713, when Colonel Irwin was still a young man and just home from the wars.

4. **Hewlett** (p.12)
Nothing is known of the subject of this tune.

5. **Máire Dhall** (**Blind Mary**) (p.13)
Composed in honour of Máire Dhall, a harper who is mentioned in Charles O'Conor's diaries as having taught his brothers Owen and Matthew at Knockmore, three miles away from their home at Belnagare, Co. Roscommon, in October 1726. This is to be performed in the so-called *sean-nós* style of a traditional Irish singer. I would strongly recommend listening carefully to the associated recording on *The Carolan Albums*.

6. **Lord Inchiquin** (p.14)
In 1543, the chief of the O'Briens, an ancient kingly Gaelic family, surrendered his chieftainship, which he held under Irish law, to Henry VIII, in return for the title of Lord Inchiquin, which was held under the English feudal system and thus descended by primogeniture. He and his descendants proved themselves to be ruthless supporters of the monarchy in the wars of the Irish with the English. During the Cromwellian campaign in Ireland, the sixth Earl of Inchiquin pursued a scorched-earth policy towards his fellow Gaels in Munster, so that he is still remembered as *Murchadh na dTóiteán* - Murrough of the Burnings. The Lord Inchiquin for whom this tune was composed, was a descendant of Murrough. The family seat was Dromoland Castle, Co. Clare, now a hotel.

7. **Morgan Magan** (p.15)
Composed for Morgan Magan of Togherstown, Co. Westmeath, who died in 1738.

8. **Sí Bheag's Sí Mhór** (The Little Fairy Hill & The Big Fairy Hill) (pp. 16 - 17)
Daniel Early's MS. Life of Carolan tells us that when Carolan set out from his home in Alderford at the age of twenty-one with the intention of establishing his career as a harper, his first place of call was the house of George Reynolds at Letterfian, Co. Leitrim. It was Reynolds - himself an amateur harper and poet, like many Irish gentlemen of the time - who suggested as a subject for composition a legendary battle between the fairy hosts of two neighbouring hills: this attractive air, Carolan's first composition, was the result.

COLONEL JOHN IRWIN
(Planxty Irwin)

Turlough O'Carolan (1670 - 1738)
Trad. arr. © 1985 Máire Ní Chathasaigh

© 1985 Máire Ní Chathasaigh

© 1985 Máire Ní Chathasaigh

HEWLETT

Turlough O'Carolan (1670 - 1738)
Trad. arr. © 1977 Máire Ní Chathasaigh

© 1977 Máire Ní Chathasaigh

BLIND MARY
(Máire Dhall)

Turlough O'Carolan (1670 - 1738)
Trad. arr. © 1979 Máire Ní Chathasaigh

© 1979 Máire Ní Chathasaigh

LORD INCHIQUIN

Turlough O'Carolan (1670 - 1738)
Trad. arr. © 1991 Máire Ní Chathasaigh

© 1991 Máire Ní Chathasaigh

MORGAN MAGAN

Turlough O'Carolan (1670 - 1738)
Trad. arr. © 1978 Máire Ní Chathasaigh

© 1978 Máire Ní Chathasaigh

SHEEBEG & SHEEMORE
(Sí Bheag 's Sí Mhór)

Turlough O'Carolan (1670 - 1738)
Trad. arr. © 1978 Máire Ní Chathasaigh

© 1978 Máire Ní Chathasaigh

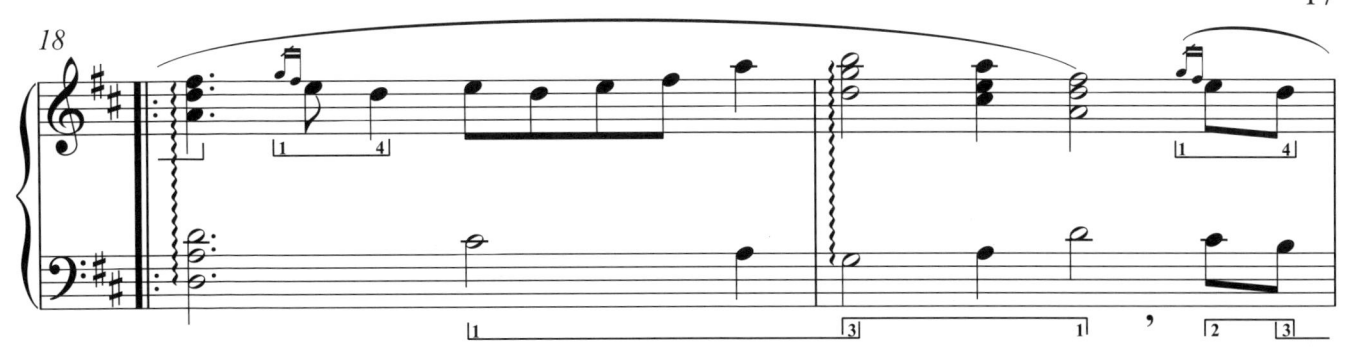
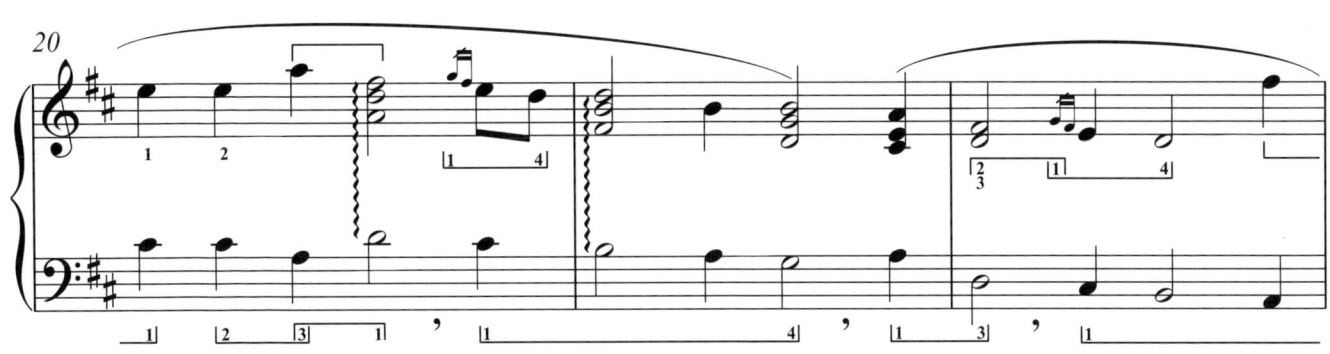
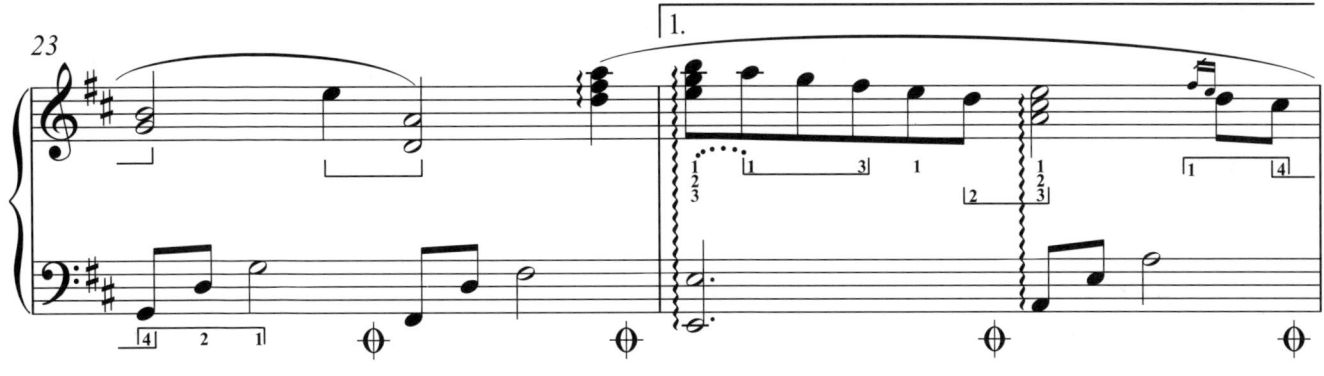

© 1978 Máire Ní Chathasaigh

THE PRINCESS ROYAL
(Miss MacDermott)

Turlough O'Carolan (1670 - 1738)
Trad. arr. © 1990 Máire Ní Chathasaigh

© 1990 Máire Ní Chathasaigh

JOHN DRURY

Turlough O'Carolan (1670 - 1738)
Trad. arr. © 1991 Máire Ní Chathasaigh

© 1991 Máire Ní Chathasaigh

FANNY POWER

Turlough O'Carolan (1670 - 1738)
Trad. arr. © 1980 Máire Ní Chathasaigh

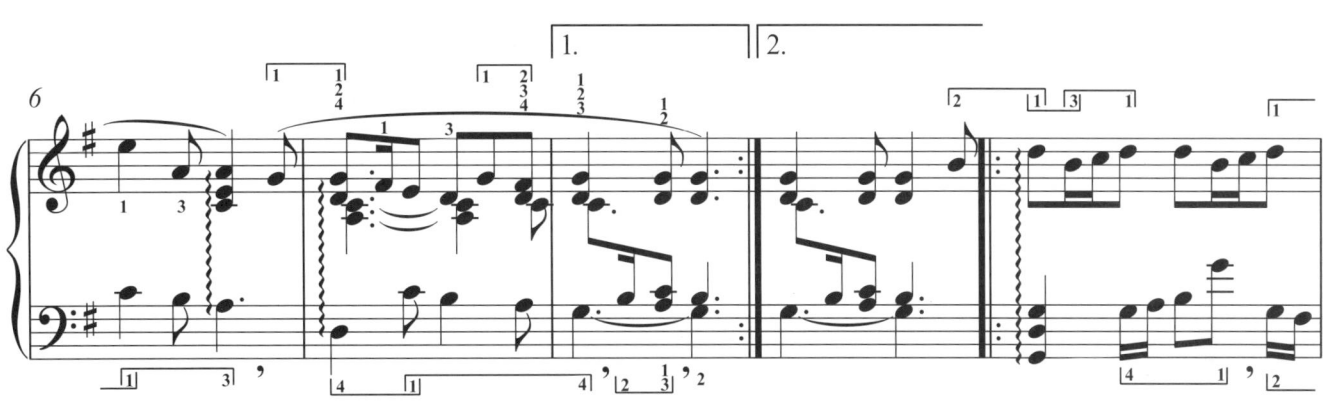
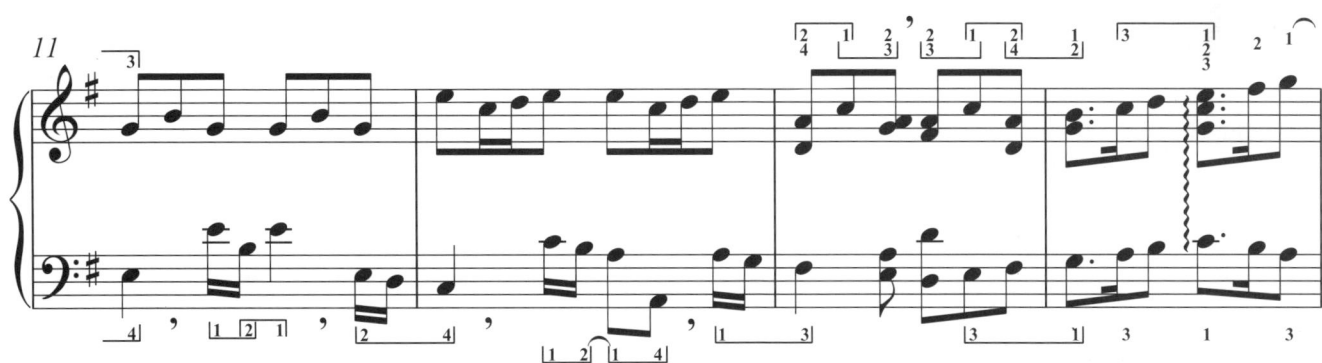

© 1980 Máire Ní Chathasaigh

CAROLAN'S CONCERTO
(Mrs. Power)

Turlough O'Carolan (1670 - 1738)
Trad. arr. © 1991 Máire Ní Chathasaigh

© 1991 Máire Ní Chathasaigh

© 1991 Máire Ní Chathasaigh

MAURICE O'CONNOR

Turlough O'Carolan (1670 - 1738)
Trad. arr. © 1994 Máire Ní Chathasaigh

© 1994 Máire Ní Chathasaigh

CONSTANTINE MAGUIRE

Turlough O'Carolan (1670 - 1738)
Trad. arr. © 1994 Máire Ní Chathasaigh

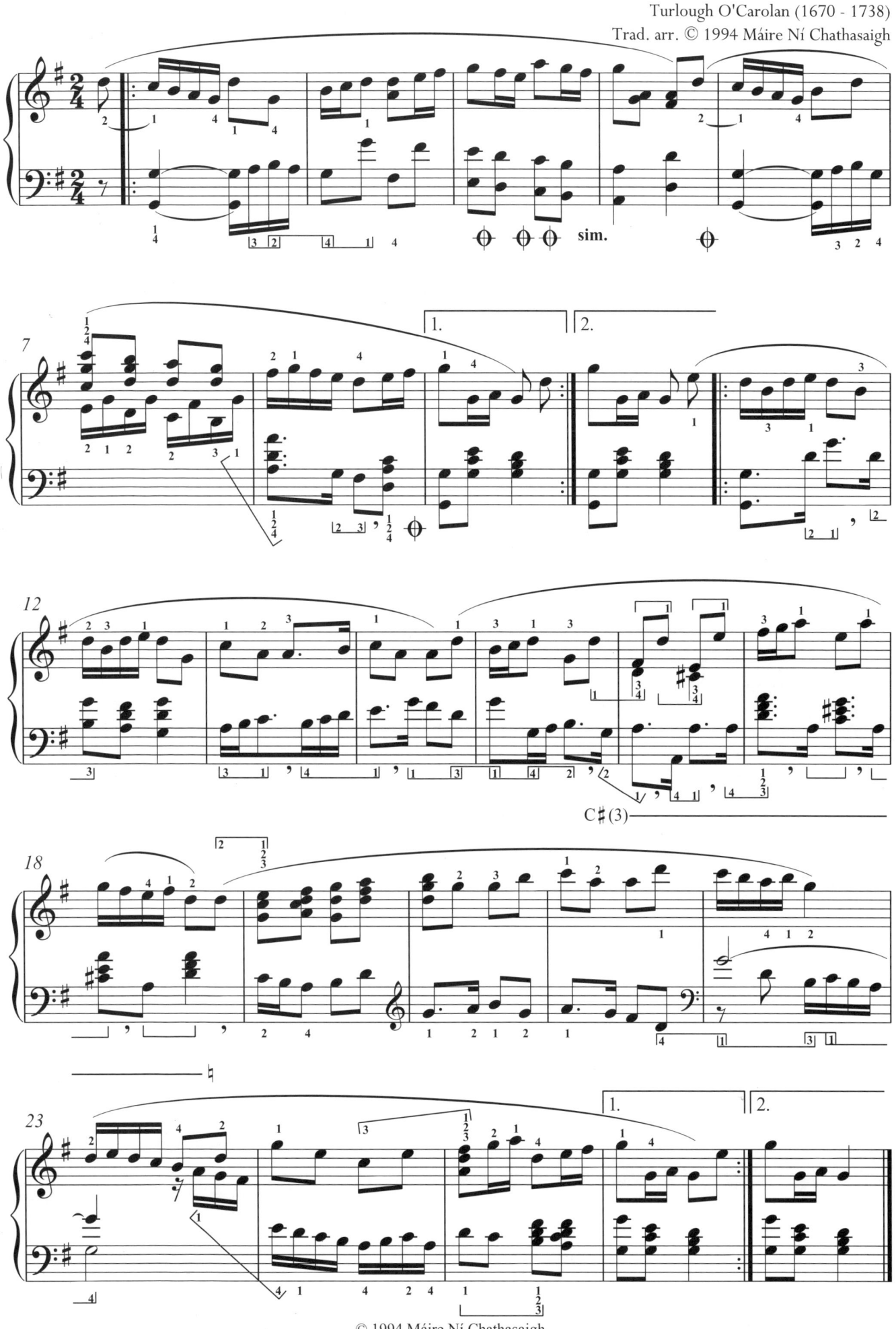

© 1994 Máire Ní Chathasaigh

MR O'CONNOR
(Part I)

Turlough O'Carolan (1670 - 1738)
Trad. arr. © 1994 Máire Ní Chathasaigh

© 1994 Máire Ní Chathasaigh

JIG
(Part II of Mr O'Connor)

© 1994 Máire Ní Chathasaigh

9. **The Princess Royal** (pp.18 - 19)
Collected by Bunting from Arthur O'Neill in 1800. Carolan composed the tune for the daughter of The MacDermott, Prince of Coolavin. *The Princess Royal* is one of the most famous of Carolan's compositions, largely because of its association with the words of the song *The Arethusa*, to which it was set by William Shield in the late eighteenth century. (The song originally appeared in a small opera or musical entertainment by Shield called *The Lock and Key*, which was first performed in 1796: it recounts the story of the engagement between the *Arethusa* and the French frigate *La Belle Poule* in the English Channel on the 17th of June 1778.) See also the notes to **John O'Connor**.

10. **John Drury** (**Planxty Drury**) (p.20)
On the 3rd of May 1724 Elizabeth Goldsmith, first cousin to the celebrated playwright Oliver Goldsmith, was married to John Drury of Kingsland, near Boyle, Co. Roscommon. This sparkling jig-like tune was composed on the occasion of the wedding. (Obtained by Bunting from Charles Byrne.) I've ornamented the tune in the manner of a traditional jig from the oral tradition.

11. **Fanny Power** (p.21)
Fanny (Frances) was the daughter and heiress of David & Elizabeth Power of Coorheen, Loughrea, Co. Galway. She married Richard Trench in 1732; their eldest son was created Earl of Clancarty in 1803. The piece must have been composed before her marriage, because in the second verse Carolan says: *"Nár fháguidh mé an saoghal go raibh mé go h-acmhuinneach A' damhsa go h-aerach is mé ar a bainis-se"* - i.e., he hopes that he will live to dance merrily at her wedding. (Collected by Bunting from Arthur O'Neill in 1800.)

12. **Carolan's Concerto** (pp.22 - 23)
A piece very much influenced by the Italian style. It was probably composed in honour of Elizabeth Power. Fanny Power, the subject of the previous tune, was her daughter. (Noted by Bunting from Arthur O'Neill.)

13. **Maurice O'Connor** (p.24)
Maurice O'Connor was the head, in Carolan's day, of the O'Connors of Offaly (see the notes to **John O'Connor**). He can't have had much money, since his ancestral lands were escheated by the attainder of his father after the Battle of Aughrim. He therefore left Ireland for England around 1700, became a member of the Inner Temple - having become nominally a Protestant for this purpose, Catholics being excluded by the Penal Laws from the legal profession - and made a fortune at the English Bar. He invested it wisely and in 1720 owned a large part of Tunbridge Wells. Soon afterwards he sold the whole of his English estates at a handsome profit and returned to Ireland. He married c.1725 Lady Mary Plunkett, youngest daughter of the 4th Earl of Fingall and a member of one of Ireland's foremost Catholic families, and acquired Coote Hall, near Boyle, Co Roscommon, from the Coote family. (Lady Mary's eldest sister Margaret had married Grace Nugent's brother John in 1720.) The present song of Carolan's celebrates this transfer of property, and expresses the general delight which it occasioned - coming so soon after the wholesale confiscations; Carolan hopes that it is a portent for the return of the dispossessed. Maurice subsequently managed to gain possession of part of his ancient inheritance in Offaly and built a new mansion there, where he died in 1740, having made several attempts to obtain leases of various parts of his family's forfeited lands, but being told that this was out of the question, as 'he might set up a title to the fee'.

14. **Constantine Maguire** (p.25)
Constantine's real name in Irish was Cúchonnnacht, a common family name among the Maguires of Tempo, Co. Fermanagh, a great and ancient Irish family. According to the family genealogy, our Cúchonnacht's grandfather, Cúchonnacht Mór Maguidhir, the head of his family, "mortgaged the greatest part of his estates to raise and arm a regiment for the service of King James the Second. He, with his brave men, fought desperately at the Pass of Aughrim [1691], and was, with his regiment, cut to pieces, after having nearly destroyed the 2nd regiment of British Horse..." The Tempo property was escheated to the Crown by reason of his adherence to King James II, but his eldest son Brian, Constantine's father, succeeded in redeeming it: hence the family were still in possession of their estates in Carolan's time. Constantine's mother Bridget was a sister to **Grace Nugent**. He died unmarried in 1739.

15. **Mr O'Connor** (pp.26 - 28)
This tune is found in one source only - the fragment in the National Library of Ireland now thought to be part of the 1748 publication by Carolan's son of his father's music. It is my opinion that bars 17 & 18 of the published version (counted as such if the erroneously repeated bar 14 is ignored) are musically defective and therefore cannot be correct. I've therefore felt free to change them in order to create a better musical shape at this crucial point in the melody. Jig tailpieces are appended to this tune, to **Madam Judge** and to some other Carolan compositions; several others may have had similar tailpieces that have become separated from them.

ROBERT JORDAN

Turlough O'Carolan (1670 - 1738)
Trad. arr. © 1994 Máire Ní Chathasaigh

© 1994 Máire Ní Chathasaigh

BRIDGET CRUISE

Turlough O'Carolan (1670 - 1738)
Trad. arr. © 1994 Máire Ní Chathasaigh

© 1994 Máire Ní Chathasaigh

FRANK PALMER

Turlough O'Carolan (1670 - 1738)
Trad. arr. © 1994 Máire Ní Chathasaigh

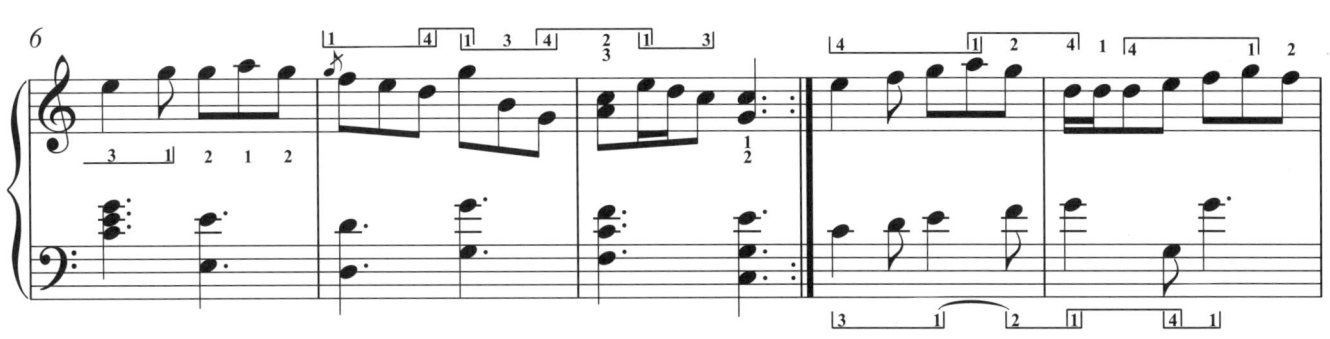
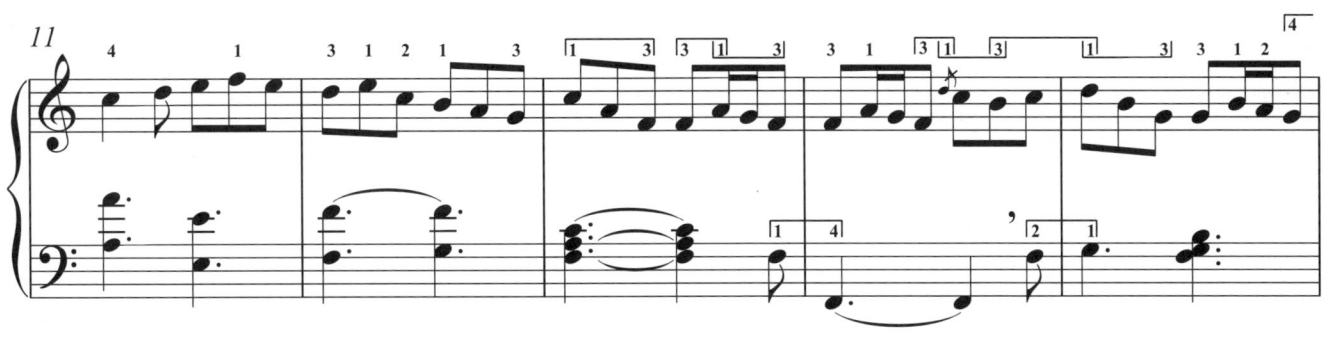

© 1994 Máire Ní Chathasaigh

D.C.

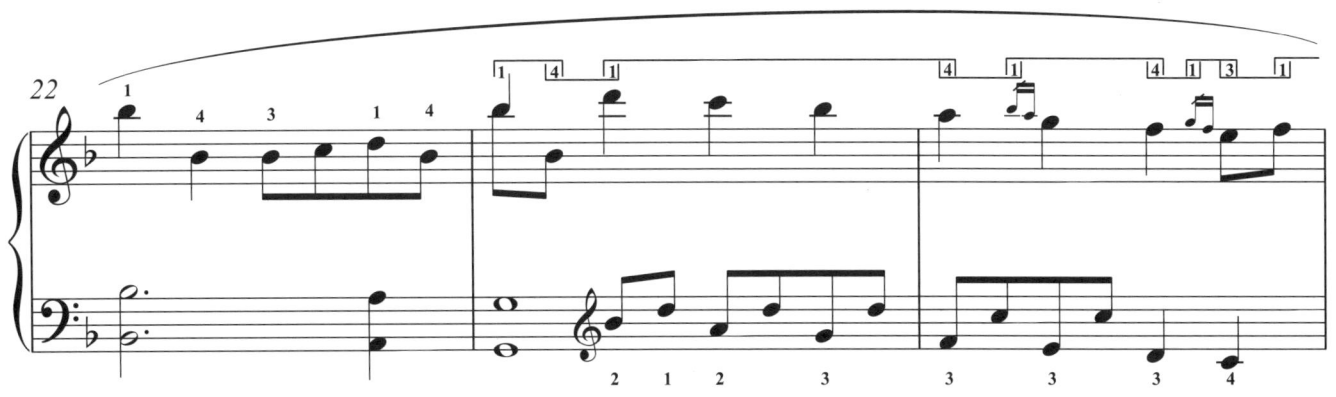
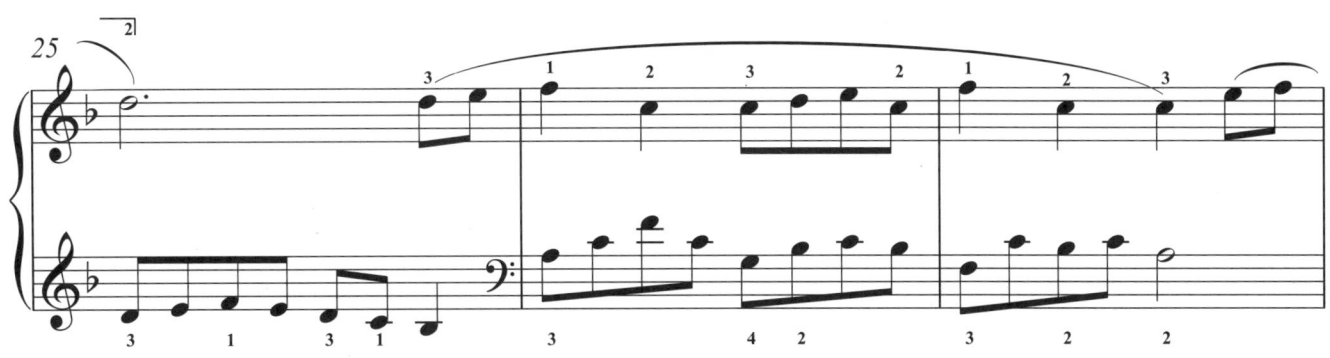
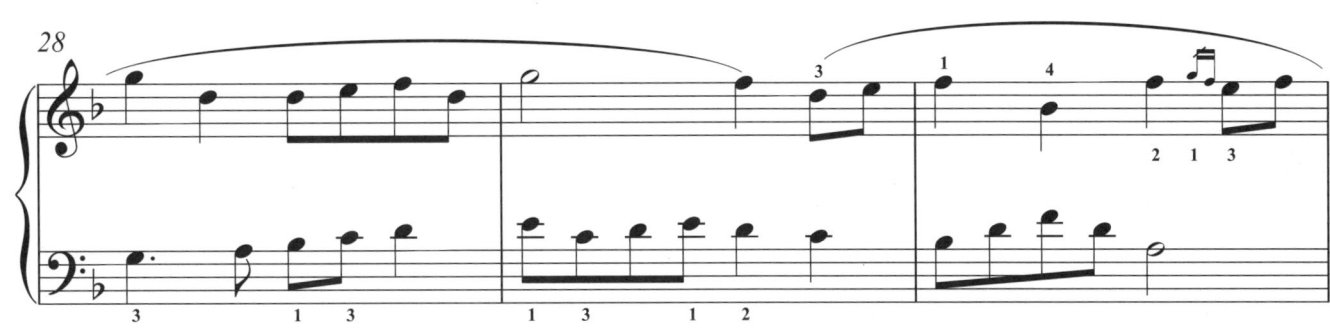

rit. and decresc. on repeat

© 1994 Máire Ní Chathasaigh

D.C.

GEORGE BRABAZON

Turlough O'Carolan (1670 - 1738)
Trad. arr. © 1994 Máire Ní Chathasaigh

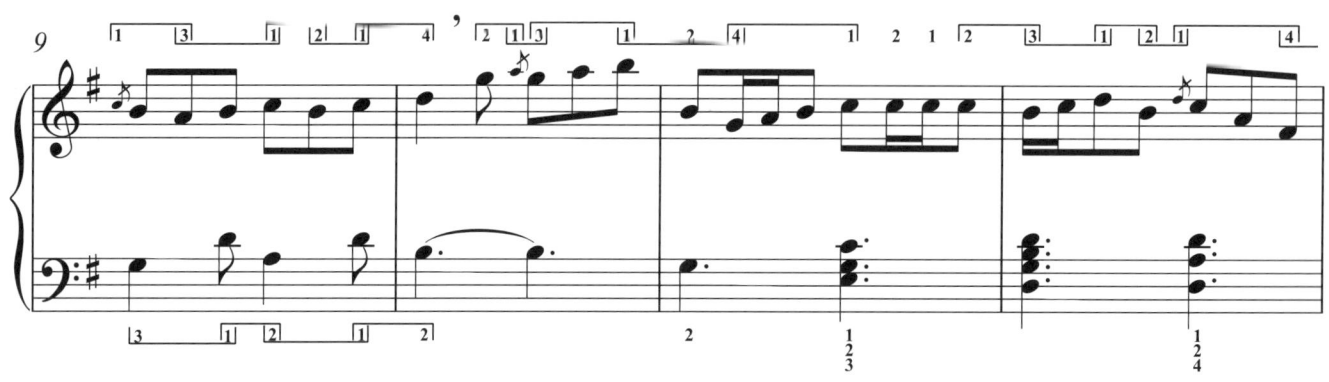

© 1994 Máire Ní Chathasaigh

MADAM JUDGE

Turlough O'Carolan (1670 - 1738)
Trad. arr. © 1994 Máire Ní Chathasaigh

ELEANOR PLUNKETT

Turlough O'Carolan (1670 - 1738)
Trad. arr. © 1994 Máire Ní Chathasaigh

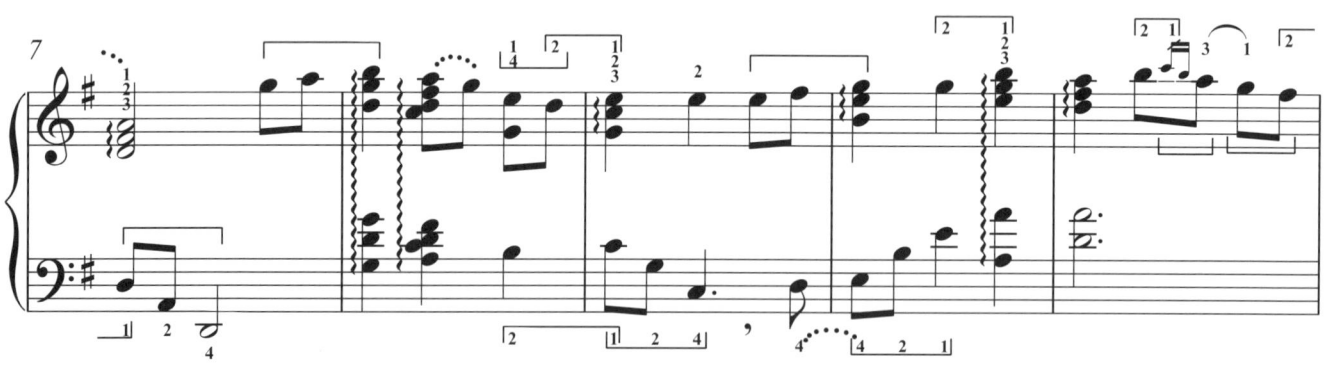

© 1994 Máire Ní Chathasaigh

BAPTIST JOHNSON

Turlough O'Carolan (1670 - 1738)
Trad. arr. © 1994 Máire Ní Chathasaigh

© 1994 Máire Ní Chathasaigh

16. **Robert Jordan** (pp.30 - 31)
Noted by Bunting from the harper Charles Fanning. Robert Jordan was a Co. Mayo landowner.

17. **Bridget Cruise** (p.32)
The tune as played here is a very beautiful and musicianly reconstruction by Dónal O'Sullivan of the imperfect MS. version collected by Forde from Hugh O'Beirne. (The arrangement is of course my own.)

Bridget Cruise was Carolan's first love and he composed several songs for her. The remains of Cruisetown House lie about two miles from Nobber, Co. Meath. It is said that Carolan fell in love with Bridget Cruise before he became blind; this is almost certainly true, since he and she were neighbours in their youth and Carolan did not contract the smallpox that blinded him until after he had moved to Co. Roscommon with his family.

Charles O'Connor relates a touching story of Carolan's attachment to Bridget Cruise, which happened many years after Carolan had left Co. Meath. In the course of a pilgrimage to St. Patrick's Purgatory (a cave on an island in Lough Dearg, Co. Donegal) while helping some other travellers into the boat needed to reach the island, Carolan happened to take a lady's hand. He instantly exclaimed, *"Dar láimh mo cháirdis Críost* (i.e., by the hand of my godfather), this is the hand of Bridget Cruise!" He was not deceived: the lady was indeed Bridget Cruise.

18. **Frank Palmer** (p.33)
This piece was in fact composed for three people, all of whom are mentioned: Roger Palmer and his wife Mary of Palmerstown, Co. Mayo, who were married c.1717-24, and their son and heir Francis. I've ornamented the tune in the manner of a traditional jig from the oral tradition.

19. **Grace Nugent** (pp.34 - 35)
Grace was the youngest daughter of James Nugent of Castle Nugent, Co. Westmeath. This tune was composed for her when she was on a visit some time before 1708 to her sister Elizabeth, who had married a Major Francis Conmee and lived at Kingsland, near Boyle, Co. Roscommon. Grace herself later married her Co. Westmeath neighbour Edward Crofton. Her youngest brother John became the head of the family when her three eldest brothers, like many Irish Catholics of good family, were "killed in the Emperor's service" in Europe. He married Lady Margaret Plunkett, eldest daughter of the 4th Earl of Fingall, in 1720; Lady Margaret's sister Mary married **Maurice O'Connor**. Grace was an aunt to **Constantine Maguire**.

20. **George Brabazon** (p.36)
Composed for George Brabazon of New Park (later called Brabazon Park) in the parish of Kilconduff, Co. Mayo. It's clear from the words that he was a young man when this song was composed for him, probably towards the end of Carolan's life. He died in 1780. I've ornamented the tune in the manner of a traditional jig from the oral tradition.

21. **Kean O'Hara** (p.37)
Composed for Kean O'Hara or Cian Ó h-Eaghra c.1657 - 1719 of Nymphsfield, Co. Sligo, Sheriff of Sligo in 1703 and 1713. Since the words of the poem are quite jolly, the tune is usually played in a similar fashion; I prefer however to interpret the tune in a more contemplative manner. You can take your choice!

22. **Madam Judge** (pp.38 - 39)
Composed for Abigail Judge of Grangebeg, Co. Westmeath. Her husband Thomas, whom she married in 1707, became High Sheriff of Leitrim and later of Westmeath. Bunting noted the first part of the tune from the harper Daniel Black, and the Jig from Hugh Higgins. A version of the first part of this tune was published in Thomson's *Select Collection of Original Irish Airs*, vol. II (1816), arranged by Beethoven.

23. **Eleanor Plunkett** (p.40)
Eleanor Plunkett, of Robertstown, Co. Meath, was the last of her family. Carolan refers to this in the second verse of the associated poem: *"Gidh nach maireann insa tír-sa Ach thú do do ghaolta"* ("Though there survives in this land Only you of your kindred"). The ruins of Robertstown House and Robertstown Castle lie just south of Cruisetown House near Nobber, Co. Meath.

24. **Baptist Johnston** (p.41)
Baptist Johnston, of Tully, Co. Monaghan, was High Sheriff of that county in 1728 and M.P. for the borough of Monaghan from 1747 until 1753, the year of his death. Bunting collected this tune from Charles Byrne. I've ornamented the tune more or less in the manner of a traditional jig from the oral tradition.

THE CAROLAN ALBUMS

Máire Ní Chathasaigh & Chris Newman
Irish Harp & Acoustic Guitar

Compact Disc   OBMCD06

All the harp arrangements in the present book can be heard on this critically acclaimed 66-minute CD. All CDs and books can be ordered from our website www.oldbridgemusic.com

"A masterpiece of virtuosity... A must for any folk-related collection." - **The Daily Telegraph**

"If Máire Ní Chathasaigh wasn't around, Irish harping would be so much the poorer... Her work, which goes beyond mere harp performance, could be described as an attempt to restore the harp to its true voice... (Here) harp and guitar partner each other in arrangements which leave conventional accompaniment far behind in their precision and attention to the finest detail. Unfussy, with all the spaces left empty and resonating, the long arm of the music reaches back into a noble tradition." - Nuala O'Connor in **The Irish Times**

"A cocktail to delight and intoxicate! Faultlessly played, with consummate skill and a perfect understanding of the grace and elegance of the music. Guitar complements harp beautifully, at times sounding almost harp-like... Máire's playing is truly breathtaking. Her deep understanding of the music, combined with technical skill and passion mark her out as the foremost modern interpreter of Carolan." - **Taplas**

"A delight... The sheer excellence of the musicianship...sets standards which should be aspired to not only in this field but throughout folk music. The sleeve notes are of a comparable standard. Very strongly recommended." - **Folkwrite**

"No one else could have done justice to such a project." - **Folk NorthWest**

"A magnificent collection from two superlative musicians... in a plethora of Carolan records, this is the best." - **Folk on Tap**

"The playing of this duo exhibits a virtuosity and balance of expression combine with a simple elegance which has a reviewer running to the thesaurus in search of superlatives. Enchanting, expressive, a remarkable piece of work." - **Tykes News**

OTHER RECORDINGS BY MÁIRE NÍ CHATHASAIGH & CHRIS NEWMAN

THE LIVING WOOD
OBMCD07

Both are in the virtuoso class"
- **The Guardian**
"The folk album of 1988."
- **The Daily Telegraph**
"Extraordinary... showcases this remarkable duo's virtuosity and technical brilliance" - **Folk Roots**

LIVE IN THE HIGHLANDS
OBMCD08

"Music of fire and brilliance from the high-wire act in traditional music"
- **The Irish Times**
"Captures the essence of these two remarkable performers in a rare and priceless way. Absolutely essential." - **Folk Roots**
"Blazing guitar and dancing harp" - **Dirty Linen** (USA)

OUT OF COURT
OBMCD03

with Nollaig Casey, Liam O'Flynn, Danny Thompson and Simon Mayor
"Gloriously adventurous"
- **The Daily Telegraph**
"Displays a stunning array of techniques and moods... supreme musicianship... one of the most refreshingly innovative releases in recent years." - **Folk Roots**

DIALOGUES
OBMCD14

"A rich and breathtaking album, in which the various styles and instruments discourse together with consummate ease, grace and joy." - **Taplas** (Wales)
"A delight" - **Sing Out** (USA)
"Terrific: brilliant, beautiful, rich, virtuosic, delightful, classic, perfect! ★★★★" - **The Sunday Tribune** (Ireland)

ALSO BY MÁIRE NÍ CHATHASAIGH
THE IRISH HARPER
VOLUME ONE (1991)

28 pages; ISBN 1 873077 00 9

Suitable for intermediate to advanced students

This book was the fruit of many years' experience of teaching the traditional music of Ireland to harpers by the pioneer in the field. It represents the first attempt in print to explain the aesthetic principles that inform the idiomatic performance of this music on the harp, and to provide detailed instructions to the aspirant harper. The majority of the arrangements are of traditional Irish dance music, but also included are two songs together with some pieces by Turlough O'Carolan. Máire has recorded most of these pieces on her albums **The New Strung Harp**, **The Living Wood** and **The Carolan Albums**, and best results can be achieved by listening to the recorded versions while following the written music. Detailed instructions are given for performance and interpretation: if conscientiously followed, idiomatic and fluent results can be achieved by the harpist with little experience of this form of music.

"The most interesting & original player of our Irish Harp today" - **Derek Bell**

"Electrifying... Máire is one of those musicians who truly deserve to be described as a virtuoso" - **Folk Roots**

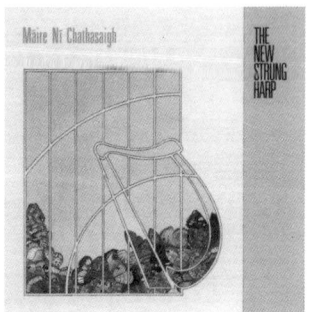

THE NEW STRUNG HARP
Temple Records COMD2019

Máire's ground-breaking solo album,
which represented the first outing on record for
the "traditional style" which she had invented for the harp

"A labour of love and a joy to the listener." - **In Dublin**

"Intensely passionate and intelligent... a milestone in Irish harp music." - **The Cork Examiner**

"Unquestionably deserves to be hailed as a classic exercise in music-making." - **The Scotsman**

"So intricate are her techniques, so subtle her use of tonal lights and shades, so inventive her arrangements, that your attention is not so much caught as captivated. She has a style all of her own but which is ideally suited to the Irish harp. Her method of ornamentation by the nimble repetition of notes adds an exhilarating skip and vigour to the dance-music... her control and timing (on slow tunes) is spellbinding... A truly beautiful album." - **Folk Roots**

"One of the loveliest albums for many a year... if you have tears to shed, prepare to shed them... The Celtic harp is not generally associated with the dancing rhythms of the reel and the hornpipe... but in Ms Ní Chathasaigh's nimble fingers the already rapid fountain of notes is further embellished by an astonishing display of decorative 'grace notes'... The whole album is practically faultless... a glorious record." - **Folk on Tap**

"I must congratulate everyone connected with the making of this marvellous album... a work of art. This is the harp album I've been waiting for: it has everything, from lively jigs and reels to slow airs and some of the best Gaelic singing you are ever likely to hear… I really can't write any more about this lovely album. In the words of a friend of mine, 'What can you say about it? It's perfect!'" - **Taplas**